ALSO BY MARY JO SALTER

Poems

A Kiss in Space (1999)
Sunday Skaters (1994)
Unfinished Painting (1989)
Henry Purcell in Japan (1985)

For Children

The Moon Comes Home (1989)

Open Shutters

Open Shutters

poems by

Mary Jo Salter

Alfred A. Knopf
New York
2005

THIS IS A BORZOI BOOK
PUBLISHED BY ALFRED A. KNOPF

Published in the United States by Alfred A. Knopf, a division of Random House, Inc., New York, and simultaneously in Canada by Random House of Canada Limited, Toronto. Distributed by Random House, Inc., New York.

www.randomhouse.com/knopf/poetry

Library of Congress Cataloging-in-Publication Data

Salter, Mary Jo.
Open shutters : poems / by Mary Jo Salter—1st ed.
p. cm.
ISBN 0-375-71014-0 (pbk)
I. Title.

PS3569.A46224 O6 2003
811'.54—dc21 2002030185

Manufactured in the United States of America

Published May 16, 2003

First Paperback Edition,
January 2005

For the three who make us four:
Brad, Emily, Hilary

Contents

Readings

PART ONE

Trompe l'Oeil

All over Genoa
you see them: windows with open shutters.
Then the illusion shatters.

But that's not true. You knew
the shutters were merely painted on.
You knew it time and again.

The claim of the painted shutter
that it ever shuts the eye
of the window is an open lie.

You find its shadow-latches strike
the wall at a single angle,
like the stuck hands of a clock.

Who needs to be correct
more often than once a day?
Who needs real shadow more than play?

Inside the house, an endless
supply of clothes to wash.
On an outer wall it's fresh

paint hung out to dry—
shirttails flapping on a frieze
unruffled by any breeze,

like the words pinned to this line.
And the foreign word is a lie:
that second *l* in *l'oeil*

which only looks like an *l*, and is silent.

The Accordionist

A whining chord of warning—the Métro's version
of Concert A—and we clear the sliding doors.
People take their seats as if assigned.
Some of them open paperbacks, like playbills,
with a formal air of expecting interruption.
Or as if the passengers themselves are actors
in a scene the stage directions might have called
Passengers reading, so that it scarcely matters
when they turn the page, or even if it's blank.

Enter a gypsy boy, who lurches forward
carrying an accordion, like a stagehand
awaiting orders where to set it down.
But when the doors wheeze shut, as if by reflex
his accordion too collapses, opens, closes
to the tune of "La Vie en Rose." He has no shoes.
Unlike the rest of us, dressed soberly
in solid colors, he's a brazen mess
of hand-me-down, ill-fitting plaids and paisleys.
He's barely old enough to be skipping school,
but no note of fear or shyness, or of shame,
shadows his face: it was years ago already
somebody taught him how to do this.

To entertain, that is—and in the coin
of the culture: an Edith Piaf song pumped
for all it's worth from the heartsore instrument
the audience links with soundtracks of old films,
as a loving camera climbs the Eiffel Tower.
But nobody is looking entertained.
They seem to be in some other kind of movie,

more modern, calling for unblinking eyes
(the actor's oldest trick for coaxing tears)
that no longer lead to tears. No words. Just chords
too grand to be specified. Or is it that?
Blank faces, maybe, standing in for blank
faces, much like wearing basic black.

The boy's still young enough he plays right through
the next stop—when he might have passed a cup—
and now, with a shrug, he segues crudely to
another chestnut: "Je Ne Regrette Rien."
My station's coming up. I start to rummage
furtively in my wallet, held as close
to heart as a hand of cards (of credit cards
luck dealt me); isolate a franc. And stand,
nearly tumbling into him, to drop
the object of my keen deliberation
into the filthy pocket of his jacket,
careful not to touch it. In a second
I stride out from the car to my next scene
on the platform, where I know to exit right
and up the stairs, out to the world of light.
I'll never see him again.

But some instinct (as the train accelerates
and howls into the tunnel on its pleated
rubber joints, one huge accordion)
tells me to look back—a backward take
on Orpheus, perhaps, in which now only
Eurydice goes free? And fleetingly

I catch through windows of the next three cars
the boy repeated. No, these are his brothers—
each with an accordion in hand
and each boy inches taller than the last—
who handed down to him these blurring clothes,
and yet because the train unreels as fast
as a movie, a single window to a frame,
my eye's confused, has fused them as one boy
growing unnaturally, an understudy
condemned to play forever underground.

Advent

Wind whistling, as it does
in winter, and I think
nothing of it until

it snaps a shutter off
her bedroom window, spins
it over the roof and down

to crash on the deck in back,
like something out of Oz.
We look up, stunned—then glad

to be safe and have a story,
characters in a fable
we only half-believe.

Look, in my surprise
I somehow split a wall,
the last one in the house

we're making of gingerbread.
We'll have to improvise:
prop the two halves forward

like an open double door
and with a tube of icing
cement them to the floor.

Five days until Christmas,
and the house cannot be closed.
When she peers into the cold

interior we've exposed,
she half-expects to find
three magi in the manger,

a mother and her child.
She half-expects to read
on tablets of gingerbread

a line or two of Scripture,
as she has every morning
inside a dated shutter

on her Advent calendar.
She takes it from the mantel
and coaxes one fingertip

under the perforation,
as if her future hinges
on not tearing off the flap

under which a thumbnail picture
by Raphael or Giorgione,
Hans Memling or David

of apses, niches, archways,
cradles a smaller scene
of a mother and her child,

of the lidded jewel-box
of Mary's downcast eyes.
Flee into Egypt, cries

the angel of the Lord
to Joseph in a dream,
for Herod will seek the young

child to destroy him. While
she works to tile the roof
with shingled peppermints,

I wash my sugared hands
and step out to the deck
to lug the shutter in,

a page torn from a book
still blank for the two of us,
a mother and her child.

The Reader

It was the morning after the hundredth birthday
of Geraldine—still quite in her right mind,
a redhead now and (people said) still pretty—
who hadn't wanted a party.

Well, if she'd lost that one, she'd stood her ground
on no singing of Happy Birthday, and no cake;
next year, with any luck, they'd learn their lesson
and not be coming back.

My friend who tells the story (a distant cousin
and a favorite, allowed to spend that night
in the nursery of the Philadelphia mansion
Geraldine was born in),

woke to the wide-eyed faces of porcelain dolls
and descended a polished winding stair that led
like a dream into the sunroom, where Geraldine
sat with the paper and read.

—Or sat with the paper lifted in her hands
like the reins of Lazarus, her long-dead horse
that had jumped a thousand hurdles; shook it once
to iron out the creases;

and kept it elevated, having been
blind for the twenty years white-uniformed,
black-skinned Edwina has been paid to stand
behind her, reading the news aloud.

The Newspaper Room

Sterling Library, Yale University

Hand-towel tabloids, editorial
bath sheets folded into the crannies
of the walk-in linen closet of knowledge!

Ever replenished, freshly washed
of whatever yesterday's forecast was—
The Asahi Shimbun, *Der Spiegel*, *The Swazi*

News, *The San Juan Star*, *The Sowetan*,
La Jornada, *The Atlanta Constitution*,
Il Tempo, *The Toronto Globe and Mail*,

Pravda, *The Age*, *The Financial Times*
(still fancifully tinted salmon)—
they're stuffed in the walls like insulation.

Consolation, too—which is odd,
because here, if you read them, are a hundred
windows open onto the howling

miseries of the day. How many
get skimmed by even one cardholder
in a week? And even when they are,

what wisdom rubs off when *The Daily*
Mirror's mirrored on the thumbs?
The one-night newsstand of the mind,

always bored the morning after, stares
blankly at the warning "To Be
Removed After Six Months." Removed

to where? To microfilm? Recycling?
The World Wide Web? The fireplace? And if
we know and hardly care, why is it

we'd feel bereft if there remained
in the universe not one such room,
relic itself of a lost age

when people hand-carved wooden shelves
with useless, newsless decoration?
Why should we relish solid proof

these pages are our days that turn
away to leave the past in ashes,
most of it local and unread?

No, she does no harm in her armchair,
that woman curled in a ball, for whom
the whole world is *Le Monde*.

TWA 800

Months after it had plummeted off the coast
  of Long Island, and teams of divers scoured
the ocean floor for blasted puzzle pieces
  to hoist and reassemble like
a dinosaur (all human cargo lost,
  too shattered to restore to more
    than names), I heard my postcard

to friends in France had been delivered at last.
  Slipped in a padded bag, with a letter
from the U.S. Postal Service ("apologies
  for any inconvenience caused
by the accident"), and sea-soaked but intact,
  it was legible in every word
    I'd written ("Looking forward

to seeing you!") and on the stamp I'd pressed
  into a corner: "Harriet Quimby,
Pioneer Pilot." Under her goggled helmet,
  she was smiling like a hostess at
this fifty-cent anecdote, in which the most
  expendable is preserved and no
    rope's thrown to the rest.

Erasers

As punishment, my father said, the nuns
   would send him and the others
out to the schoolyard with the day's erasers.

Punishment? The pounding symphony
   of padded cymbals clapped
together at arm's length overhead

(a snow of vanished alphabets and numbers
   powdering their noses
until they sneezed and laughed out loud at last)

was more than remedy, it was reward
   for all the hours they'd sat
without a word (except for passing notes)

and straight (or near enough) in front of starched
   black-and-white Sister Martha,
like a conductor raising high her chalk

baton, the only one who got to talk.
   Whatever did she teach them?
And what became of all those other boys,

poor sinners, who had made a joyful noise?
   My father likes to think,
at seventy-five, not of the white-on-black

chalkboard from whose crumbled negative
those days were never printed,
but of word-clouds where unrecorded voices

gladly forgot themselves. And that he still
can say so, though all the lessons,
most of the names, and (he doesn't spell

this out) it must be half the boys themselves,
who grew up and dispersed
as soldiers, husbands, fathers, now are dust.

Tanker

On the horizon
One toy tanker pitches south
Playing hide and seek.

Broad as a fan, each rust-pocked
Leaf of the sea-grape.

—from "Fort Lauderdale," by James Merrill

Almost a tanka—
Which (to remind the reader)
Allows a haiku

To glide above two submerged
Lines of seven syllables.

———

In my living room
Seven years after your death,
As a tape gave back

Your suave, funny-sad voice, I
Suddenly understood it.

———

"Toy tanker," of course!
You'd pruned the tanka's final
Syllables to five.

No one but you would have made
a bonsai of a bonsai.

———

The tanka I cite
Is the *Mirabell* of three:
A toy trilogy.

Florida: last stop before
The grandeur of Sandover?

You played hide-and-seek—
Hoping a few fans might take
A leaf from your book.

Glimpsed behind the geisha's fan:
Your quick smile, eyebrows lifted.

Some people make real
Tankers that can transport oil,
Do the heavy stuff.

Your father was one of them.
He greased your way: God bless him.

Why count syllables
When half the world is hungry?
You had no answer,

Planted another sea-grape
In bright rows, ornamental.

———

How many poems
Take the disappearing ship
As death's vehicle!

Distant, you remain in view,
Still running on drops of ink.

Glasses

Tattooed, goateed, burly, a huge
guy you'd expect to find in a hardhat,
   drilling a hole in the road,

he pulls out from his T-shirt pocket
a crumpled, quietly crafted page
   in praise of a fellow poet.

Then steps up to the podium, slips
his glasses on, and everything blurs.
   Sorry, he laughs, *they're hers—*

these glasses are my wife's. I've met
his wife. She's blond, fine-boned, serene,
   with a face you'd swear was painted

five hundred years ago by Van Eyck.
Don't worry, he's chuckling into the mike,
I've found my own. But his tone
   is a little disappointed.

Hare

At odd times, harum-scarum,
after we haven't seen him
for a week or so, he hops
from the bushes at stage right
onto our green proscenium.

Why do I say it's ours?
At best, I'm just a warden,
standing with hands in suds
at the kitchen window when
he breaks out of his warren.

Jittery, hunted vagrant,
he leaps as fast as Aesop
claimed his kind could leap,
then stops still in the grass
merely because it's fragrant—

a wholly interested,
systematic sensualist,
a silent, smooth lawn mower
that hardly can go slower.
Sometimes he gets ahead

(or tries to) with the jet set,
in a long line at the airport
pulling his legs behind him
like luggage, bit by bit—
the nametag of his scut

attached at the last minute.
Meanwhile, I stay put
inside the house we bought
a year ago, a new
woman at the window—

but of that he has no clue,
now pawn, now skipping knight
on sun-squares on the lawn,
while dreaming the old dream
a hare has, of his harem.

Is he in fact the same
animal all the time?
In my way promiscuous
as he, how could I swear
he's not some other hare

that pauses blank-eyed, poses
as if for praise, and then,
rather than jump over,
inserts himself within
a low bush, like a lover?

Both of us bad at faces,
mere samples of our species,
will either of us be missed?
The dishes in my hands
are shards for the archeologist.

In the Guesthouse

1. LONG EXPOSURE, 1892

All of them dead by now, and posed
so stiffly, in their sepia Sunday
best, they seem half-dead already.
Father and Eldest Son, each dressed
in high-cut jacket and floppy tie,
never get to sit in the sitting room.
They stand to face a firing squad
behind Mother and the little girls—
themselves bolt upright on the sofa,
hands at their sides, their center-parted
hair pulled back, two rows of rickrack
flanking the twenty buttons down
the plumb line of their bodices.

And here, discovered alone downstage
and slightly to the left, the boy—
such a beautiful boy. Although
they've tried to make him a little man,
upholstering him in herringbone,
you can see him itching to run out
with his hoop and stick, happy because
even at this moment, when
nobody could be happy, he knows—
in the tilt of his blond head, the frank
time-burning gaze beneath his cowlick—
that he is the most loved.

2. FLAPPERS, 1925

I'm in the guesthouse some days before
focusing on another portrait:
professional, black-and-white, composed

to lend a spacious dignity
to the one life lived behind each face.
Again, the date's approximate;

I'm guessing from the arty look,
the Flapperish, drop-waisted frock
and ropes of wooden beads on the wife

of—yes, it has to be. No more
the poster boy for posterity,
he's a commanding forty. The cowlick's

still there (although now he slicks
it down with something), and he still
cocks his head to one side, a hint

of flirtation, exasperation—what?—
in the eyes he trains at the camera
as if he'd give me what I want

if only he could emerge now from
the frame. We stare in mutual
boldness while his wife's long profile

is tendered to the child between them.
One girl: a modern family.
I speculate a little son

was lost to the great flu; even so,
this fair-haired Zelda in a bob,
ten years old, would come to seem

enough, the image of her father.
The smile high-cheeked and confident,
the shining eyes, the upturned chin—

people matter more now; they'll die
less often, now that the Great War's over;
everyone's allowed to sit down.

3. WHEELCHAIR, 2000

The jumbles of grinning faces jammed
together at birthdays and Christmases
in color photos around the house
   don't interest me.

They're merely *today*, or close enough;
anybody can record it
and does; if everything's recorded
   nothing is.

But puttering about, the guest
of a ghost I now am half in love with,
I'm drawn one day to pluck one image
  off the piano.

A wedding. Or some minutes after,
outside a church I've seen in town.
The bride, who has exercised her right
  to veil, white gown,

and any decorum life affords
these days, is surrounded by the girls—
some floral aunts, a gawky niece
  in her first pearls—

and all the men in blazers, khakis . . .
running shoes? Boys will be boys.
Squirming, they squint into the sun:
  some amateur

shutterbug has made sure they can't
see us, or we see them, and yet
I understand now who is shaded
  there in the wheelchair.

Dwindled, elderly, it's Zelda—
her lumpy little body slumped
like a doll's in a high chair, shoes just
  grazing the footrest.

It must be she. However many
lives her hair went through—Forties
complications held with tortoise-
  shell combs; beehives;

softer bouffants like Jackie's; fried
and sprayed gray-pincurl granny perms—
in all the years (say, seventy-five?)
  since I last saw her,

she's come back to that sleek, side-parted
bob, which (though it's white) encloses
the girl who's smiling, pert, high-cheeked,
  despite the pull

of gravity: just like her father.
Or as he was. *When did he die,*
and how? What was his name? What's yours?
  I could find out,

surely, when I leave here; the owner
might well be her granddaughter.
I could scout, too, for snapshots even
   more recent—some

get-together with no wheelchair—
to prove what I'm sensing: Zelda's gone.
Why would they think to frame this scene,
   unless it's the last?

But why should *we* care so for people
not us or ours—recognized by sight
alone—whose voices never spoke
   with wit or comfort

to us, and whose very thoughts,
imagined, every year grow quainter?
Yet they must have felt this tug as well,
   repeatedly

peering at someone they were bound
to come back to, as in a mirror.
Who says they're more anonymous
   than I am,

packing up after my two weeks
in the guesthouse? I make one last study
of Zelda's father, lingering with
   the boy, the man,

sealing his developing
face in myself for safekeeping.
Too soon to leave. But then, nobody
   ever stays here long.

Night Thoughts

1.

The hunchback is curled
all night in my shut closet.
I am six years old.

2.

Dark in the cabin.
No lamp but the blue moon of
the computer screen.

3.

Pebbles on the beach:
the waves, without swallowing,
deliver a speech.

4.

I'd need a furnace
(if I were a glassblower)
to make icicles.

5.

She's alone in bed.
In an earlier time zone
he dines a lover.

6.

A page of haiku:
among the caught fireflies, one
lights the whole bottle.

Snowed-on Snowman

"Want to make a snowman?"
—So goes her wide-eyed question
on a Sunday in January.
I've been sweeping the kitchen floor
and prop the broom, like a bookmark,
against the vertical line
that joins one wall to another.
I check my watch: 3:30.
The last light of the weekend,
her last such invitation,
maybe: she's thirteen.

"I'm not sure it's packable.
It may not be good snow,
or enough snow for a snowman."
—So go my instinctive,
unfun, nay-saying quibbles:
I've been an adult a long time.

"Could we make a snowchild then?"
Straight-faced, without guile,
she doesn't seem to know
she's just invented a word—
or that its snow-fresh sound
compels the thing's creation.

Seize the day in a snowball
and roll it across the yard;
leave a paper-thin
membrane between winter

and a spring that's coming up
in clumps of grass and soil;
roll the ball rounder, bigger,
make a second, a third,
then pile them, roughly centered,
one on top of the other,
like marshmallows on a stick.

And human, for all that:
remarkable how little
skill it takes to make us
believe in, fall in love with,
this lopsided Galatea
(and why do we say it's male?
Why do we feel that poking
a tarnished candle-snuffer
for a pipe in his mouthless head
will finally clinch the matter?).

Dressed, at last, in every
cliché we can think of—scarf
wrapped against the cold
of himself, a wide-brimmed hat
shielding his unshelled
almond eyes and carrot
nose from a burning snowlight
ruddied by low sun—
he's readier than she
(reverting, herself, to pure
put-upon type, the impatient

teenager) to pose
for a snapshot side by side—
each soon to disappear,
him shrinking as she grows.

But not before Monday morning.
Slipping out to hunt
the rolled-up paper, dreading
along with it the widespread
old news of Sunday's snow
gone smudged, a little yellow,
I find instead a fine
life-dust on everything:

snow on the snowman's hat
(whose brim serves to define
the line between what's molded
by us, and snow like that);
snow too light to burden
his rounded back or shoulders,
or mine, the shoveler's;
snow like breakfast crumbs
I nearly brush from his scarf
before I catch myself.

Inside, I stamp my boots
and call upstairs. *You're late*,
I usually say; *you must*
eat your toast, *it's getting cold*;

how can you take an hour
to decide which jeans to wear?
In a corner, the forgotten
broom still marks the place
of yesterday in the room.
"Come down," I call up again.
"Come see the snowed-on snowman."

Light-Footed

AN INTERLUDE

Deliveries Only

for Sarah Marjorie Lyon, born in a service elevator

Your whole life long, you'll dine
out on the same questions:
In your building? On what floor?
Was it going up or down?

They'll need the precise location—
Seventy-ninth and Lex?—
as if learning it could shield them
from the consequences of sex.

Wasn't your mother a doctor?
Didn't she talk him through
how to do it? And then you'll tell them
how your father delivered you,

that only after your birth
did he think to reach in her bag
and dial 911.
He held you up like a phone

and was taught how to cut the cord.
What about proper hygiene?
When did the ambulance come?
Waiting, you were the siren,

squalling in a rage
behind the old-fashioned mesh
of the elevator door:
a Lyon cub in her cage.

Didn't your parents worry?
Hadn't they done Lamaze?
But you'll only shrug at your story:
That was the way it was.

School Pictures

Nobody wants them, not even Mom. And Dad
always pretends they fell out of his wallet.
Not even at thirteen could we look that bad.

Maybe it's trick photography, like an ad.
We combed our hair. When did somebody maul it?
Nobody wants them, not even Mom and Dad.

No self-respecting kid would wear that plaid.
She looks so Eighties in that whatchamacallit.
Not even at thirteen could we look that bad.

Say cheese at 9 a.m.? Jeez, we were mad.
But we meant to please the public, not appall it.
Nobody wants them. Not even Mom and Dad,

homely as they are, have ever had
a girl you might mistake for Tobias Smollett.
Not even at thirteen could we look that bad.

We could try to call it art, the latest fad,
but could we find a gallery to install it?
Nobody wants them, not even Mom and Dad.
Not even at thirteen could we look that bad.

A Morris Dance

Across the Common, on a lovely May
day in New England, I see and hear
the Middle Ages drawing near,
bells tinkling, pennants bright and gay—
   a parade of Morris dancers.

One plucks a lute. One twirls a cape.
Up close, a lifted pinafore
exposes cellulite, and more.
O why aren't they in better shape,
   the middle-aged Morris dancers?

Already it's not hard to guess
their treasurer—her; their president—him;
the Wednesday night meetings at the gym.
They ought to practice more, or less,
   the middle-aged Morris dancers.

Short-winded troubadours and pages,
milkmaids with osteoporosis—
what really makes me so morose is
how they can't admit their ages,
   the middle-aged Morris dancers.

Watching them gamboling and tripping
on Maypole ribbons like leashed dogs,
then landing, thunderously, on clogs,
I have to say I feel like skipping
   the middle-aged Morris dancers.

Yet bunions and receding gums
have humbled me; I know my station
as a member of their generation.
Maybe they'd let me play the drums,
  the middle-aged Morris dancers.

Office Hours

Unlock the door, drop my backpack,
turn the computer on, and the kettle;
waiting for both to warm up, settle
behind the unfilable disaster
of my cabinet, and ignore that stack
  on the floor since last semester.

What a strange job I have—supplying
people with meter and metaphors!
I could be trying to write poems.
Instead, I've tried improving yours—
the ones about your grandmothers dying,
  your cats, your broken homes,

your clueless junior years in Europe;
vainly I've tried to quash the onset
of another sonnet on a sunset.
Commencement Day should make me cheer up;
and although today I feel elated
  a pack of you graduated

(the few who slaved to get a summa,
the hundreds who will die not knowing
the proper placement of the comma),
I must admit that, watching caps
and gowns go by, I had a lapse
  in judgment: I was growing

sorry to lose—well, two of you.
Funny, clever, and modest too,
fresh from an internship at *Glamour,*
lovely Amanda would always bring—
throughout the autumn, winter, spring—
  poems about sex last summer.

Diane was writing a Book of Hours.
Terse through her Terce, mutely applauding
her Lauds, I knew my place, at least.
Deferring to her higher powers,
behind the grille of my desk, nodding,
  I listened like a priest.

Sure, it was selfish that I booked
you both for Tuesdays at eleven,
but didn't you find to your surprise
(as I did) that fine-tuning even
projects unlike as yours soon looked
  part of one enterprise,

and to hell with "independent studies"?
To view the whole thing as a game
we'd dare to lose at; to focus on
one line until it's more than one—
yes, you *got* that, and I came
  to see you as my buddies,

who reminded me of that grand plan
I had, I think, when I was young.
You showed we could write anything
at all, if we took the time to do it.
Excuse me, Amanda and Diane,
    if I now start to get to it.

The Big Sleep

Two bodies in bed, each with a book.
"Would you mind if I turn
the light off?" I ask nicely.
"Would you mind waiting
just a few more pages?" he asks nicely;
"They just found another dead body."
(My husband is reading Raymond Chandler.)
"Sure," I say. "I understand."

So I go back to my book.
Mine is about the disastrous history
of navigation, before the solution
of the problem of longitude.
More often, *he's* reading about science,
and I'm reading fiction.
After a while I set down the book,
and behind my lids I see floaters of planets
slide and flicker—
celestial bodies, all unlabeled,
that could never guide me if I were a sailor.

My husband's the one
with the sense of direction.
(Yes, I'm aware
of the gender cliché—
but what can I do? It's true.)
Amazing what he doesn't notice—
what I'm wearing, what he's wearing,
half the things I notice.
But he can't believe I'd never dare

to experiment with a new route home;
that before reading this book, this week,
I'd always confused latitude and longitude.

For now, though, nobody's going far.
"Want me to read this aloud to you?"
he offers. "It might help you sleep."
He reads me a few pages
of snappy dialogue and guns
before I stop him.
"It's too funny," I say.
"It's too wonderful. It makes me laugh.
I'll never get to sleep."

He turns off the light—
which may mean what it does
in Raymond Chandler movies.
But soon we slide, lock, side to side,
my stomach to his back,
like continents buckling
over the rumpled waters,
and in time, although no observer
is there to report it, we probably look
like corpses, except that he always snores.
Sometimes I do. We wake each other up
a lot, and apologize,
his body and my body,
till death do us part.

Readings

PART TWO

Another Session

1.

You opened with the rules. Outside this room
nothing I said inside would be repeated
unless in your best judgment I posed harm
to myself or others. It was like being read
my rights in some film noir—but I was glad
already I'd at last turned myself in,
guilty of anxiety and depression.

And worse. Confess it: worse. Of narcissist
indifference to how other people felt.
Railing against myself, making a list
of everything (I thought), I'd left a fault
unturned: the one of needing to be praised
for forcing these indictments from my throat.
For saying them well. For speaking as I wrote.

2.

Not that the goal was chalking up demerits.
Indeed, I hoped you were basically on my side.
That's how I interpreted your nod,
your pleasant face (at first, a little hard
to judge behind that beard), your intelligent
air of listening further than I meant.
And never falsely, just to raise my spirits,
but because you couldn't not be interested.

"You writers!" When the outburst came, I started
out of my chair. (I'd had a habit then—
feet on your coffee table. Never again.)
"This is real life. You don't live in a novel.
People aren't characters. They're not a symbol."
We stared, stunned at the other, stony-hearted.

3.

Once or twice a week, for a year. But ten
years ago already, so that today
those intimate, subtle, freeform sessions shrink
to memorized refrains: "You seem to think
people can read your mind. You have to *say*"—
itself said kindly—or that time you accused me
of picturing love too much like "Barbie and Ken.
Why does it have to be all youth and beauty?"

Therapists have themes, as writers do.
(A few of mine, then: the repertoire includes
clocks, hands, untimely death, snow-swollen clouds.)
Like it or not, I picked up more from you:
No showing off. In failure, no surprise.
Gratitude. Trust. Forgiveness. Fantasies.

4.

The last time I saw your face—how far back now?—
was when I took my daughters (I still don't
know what possessed me) to a "family restaurant."
Dinosaur portions, butter enough to drown
all sorrows in, cakes melded from candy bars . . .
Having filed you away for years and years,
suddenly I was nervous, my life on show.
I'm still married, thanks. Husband's out of town.

But there was no talking to you across the aisle
where, by some predestined trick of seating,
your brood in its entirety was eating
(their dinners, I suppose, were just as vile)
with backs to me, remaining as they must
faceless to patients even from the past.

5.

Killed instantly. That's what a mutual friend
told me when I asked how it had happened.
Good, I said, *I'm glad he didn't suffer*—
each of us reaching (not far) for a phrase
from a lifetime stock of journalists' clichés
which, we had learned, provide a saving buffer
within our bifurcated selves: the one
that's horrified; the one that must go on.

Killed in a bicycle race. I've scrapped the Wheel
of Fortune, the Road of Life. No, this is real,
there's no script to consult: you've lost your body.
Still having one, I pace, I stretch, I cough,
I wash my face. But then I'm never ready.
This is the sonnet I've been putting off.

6.

And also this one, in which your fancy bike
hits a concrete barrier and you fly
over it into fast *oncoming traffic*—
the obituary's formula for one man
driving a truck, who didn't even have
time to believe the corner of his eye,
until the thing was done, and he must live
always as if this nightmare were the one
deed he was born to do and to relive,
precisely the sort of person you would trust
in fifty-minute sessions to forgive
himself, to give himself at least two years
of post-traumatic whatsit to adjust
to thoughts of all those people left in tears.

7.

Only once did you confide a story
from your own life. (And only to illustrate
how long "people" take to overcome a shock.)
An accident—you broke your neck? Your back?
Shameful I don't remember—and for three
years you'd take a detour to avoid
the sight of it: that swinging, high red light
somebody ran, that road that crossed a road.

A run-through of the sped-up, drawn-out second
of terror before your second, actual end.
Swinging past the turnoff to your clinic
today, I saw I'd never choose to drive
that street again; would steer around the panic
rather than fail to find you there alive.

8.

Notice—but you can't—I don't write your name.
People aren't characters. Here's my concession
(small) to that view, and your need of privacy
which, I suspect, went beyond your profession.
When I knew you—no, you knew *me*—I'd missed the easy
truth we had acquaintances in common.
(A good thing, probably, I'd been too dim
to ask you; you too classy to let on.)

Nor did I find the public facts in print
(*age 53, father of three, an active
member of his church*) until you'd long
been dead. That July I came and went.
You reached me in a place I don't belong—
seventeen months later, Christmas Eve.

9.

I'd got there early, casually saved a front
pew for the whole family with some flung
mittens and hats. (In gestures we assume
the shoulder-to-shoulder permanence of home.)
Shouldn't we come more often? "The Power of Love":
our sermon. A list called "Flowers in Memory of"
on the program's final page. I was feeling faint.
Your name. Your father's name? Something was wrong.

I knew it was you. The church was going black.
Head down: my first anxiety attack
since the bad old days. Your face at the restaurant.
My plate heaped up with food I didn't want.
Keep the head down. People would be saying
to themselves (and close enough) that I was praying.

10.

Revise our last encounter. I'd rather say
it was that day a decade ago we made
a formal farewell: I was going away
on a long trip. If I needed you, I said,
when I got back, I'd be sure to give a call.
You stood up, and I finally saw how tall
you were; I'd never registered how fit.
Well, all we'd done for a year was talk and sit.

Paris, you said. Then, awkwardly, *Lucky you*.
Possessor of my secrets, not a friend,
colder, closer, our link unbreakable.
Yet we parted better than people often do.
We looked straight at each other. Was that a smile?
I thanked you for everything. You shook my hand.

For Emily at Fifteen

Sirens living in silence, why would they leave the sea?
—Emily Leithauser

Allow me one more try,
though you and I both know
you're too old now to need
writing about by me—

you who composed a sonnet
and enclosed it in a letter,
casually, with family news,
while I was away;

who rummaged in convention's
midden for tools and symbols
and made with them a maiden
voyage from mere verse

into the unmapped world
of poetry. A mermaid
(like Eve, you wrote—a good
analogy, and yet

your creature acts alone)
chooses to rise from wordless
unmindful happiness
up to the babbling surface

of paradox and pain.
I whose job it's been
to protect you read my lesson:
you'll wriggle from protection.

Half-human and half-fish
of adolescence, take
my compliments, meant half
as from a mother, half

one writer to another,
for rhymes in which you bury
ironies—for instance,
sirens into *silence;*

and since I've glimpsed a shadow,
forgive how glad I felt
when I set down your sonnet
to read your letter again

with only silliness in it,
the old tenth-grade bravado:
"Oh well, I bombed the chem test.
Latin's a yawn a minute."

Midsummer, Georgia Avenue

Happiness: a high, wide porch, white columns
crowned by the crepe-paper party hats
of hibiscus; a rocking chair; iced tea; a book;
an afternoon in late July to read it,
or read the middle of it, having leisure
to mark the place and enter it tomorrow
just as you left it (knock-knock of woodpecker
keeping yesterday's time, cicada's buzz,
the turning of another page, and somewhere
a question raised and dropped, the pendulum-
swing of a wind-chime). Back and forth, the rocker
and the reading eye, and isn't half

your jittery, odd joy the looking out
now and again across the road to where,
under the lush allées of long-lived trees
conferring shade and breeze on those who feel
none of it, a hundred stories stand confined,
each to their single page of stone? Not far,
the distance between you and them: a breath,
a heartbeat dropped, a word in your two-faced
book that invites you to its party only
to sadden you when it's over. And so you stay
on your teetering perch, you move and go nowhere,
gazing past the heat-struck street that's split

down the middle—not to put too fine
a point on it—by a double yellow line.

Snowbirds

Profiles framed in the window's
glare of Florida sun,
two friends, both snow-capped widows,
are sharing a cinnamon bun.

Are they economizing?
Fearing their waists can afford
just half of that white icing?
Neither one says a word

while they divide with a knife
the whorling galaxy
of their treat, like girls at tea,
starting to play at life.

Alike impeccable
in Keds and peds and pleated
tennis shorts, they're seated
at their accustomed table—

or what feels customary
now that they needn't worry
about filling another's mouth;
now that they don't fly south

anymore, or north, or provide
eggs for anybody.
And yet our cares die hard.
One woman is still ready,

unasked, not looking up,
to pour a long white stream
from a tiny pitcher of cream
into the other's cup.

Florida Fauna

1.

Silently, the green
long-tailed lizard glides across
our floor like a queen.

2.

Who was first to spear
toothpicks through melon balls and
diced alligator?

3.

Ice cubes in a glass:
outside, the chilling shake of
rattlesnake through grass.

Discovery

6:48 a.m., and leaden
little jokes about what heroes
we are for getting up at this hour.
Quiet. The surf and sandpipers running.
T minus ten and counting, the sun
mounting over Canaveral
a swollen coral, a color
bright as camera lights. We're blind-
sided by a flash:

shot from the unseen
launching pad, and so from nowhere,
a flame-tipped arrow—no, an airborne
pen on fire, its ink a plume
of smoke which, even while zooming
upward, stays as oddly solid
as the braided tail of a tornado,
and lingers there as lightning would
if it could steal its own thunder.

—Which, when it rumbles in, leaves
under or within it a million
firecrackers going off, a thrill
of distant pops and rips in delayed
reaction, hitting the beach in fading
waves as the last glint of shuttle

receives our hands' eye-shade salute:
the giant point of all the fuss soon
smaller than a star.

Only now does a steady, low
sputter above us, a lawn mower
cutting a corner of the sky,
grow audible. Look, it's a biplane!—
some pilot's long-planned, funny tribute
to wonder's always-dated orbit
and the itch of afterthought. I swat
my ankle, bitten by a sand gnat:
what the locals call no-see-'ums.

Double Takes

THE DEBUTANTE

Heads turn: in the taffeta rustle
of leaves, clutching a dance-card
acorn under her chin,
a high-society squirrel
curls her tail like a bustle.

NORWOTTUCK

The leftward-peaking curve
of the mountain just behind
our house puts me in mind
of a huge, arrested wave
engraved upon the sky's
absorbent paper . . . wait,
that thought
was Hokusai's.

Shadow

The name of my neighbors' black Lab is Shadow.
He stands on the deck in back of their house
like a figurehead fixed on the wrong direction.
The house—across the street, at the corner—
I view from one side, as I do the dog.
Shadow faces astern while the prow
  leans into the morning sun.

Whenever I wake, my first sight is Shadow
already at military attention.
His profile's imperial, nearly Egyptian.
Turning in bed, I stare out the window,
unaware of my room, as if the glass
were my eyes, and what I see out of it
  is freighted as a dream.

But no, this is the day's first emblem
of the real, because it *is* real: a black
dog that doesn't know I'm looking
as he looks out over the back yard thinking
at whatever level he's thinking,
while I lie in silence, starting to grasp
  whatever it is I feel.

There's something cheering about him, something
comic in his erect, respectful
salute to the day; and a call to sadness—
though I resist this, not wishing to greet
my own life with less gratitude
than a dog chained to a post. What is it
  about his silhouette

that lends the whole neighborhood the flat,
deluded air of a stage set—like
a backdrop whose painted simplicity
of House and Tree only seals the fate
of the characters in the tragedy?
Besides, what's the tragedy? I'm all right,
  and so, I think, is Nancy,

who now steps out to the deck in her robe,
unhooks Shadow's leash. He follows her in.
I know what will happen next: she'll emerge
briskly in work clothes, and back the car out
past the woodpile, the trash cans, the basketball hoop,
her late summer garden; I'll watch her turn up
  the street to disappear

on the hilltop, seeming to tumble off it.
No tragedy. She'll be back at three.
Yet the thought was *there* just a moment ago,
barely within the range of my senses:
an equal consciousness
of how little I understand that the life
  one has is one's only life

and how well I understand it; and how
most of the time one functions better
forgetting. Do I want to function?
It's humbling to think that human ears
are duller than dogs'. I rise and dress,
and for better or worse the darkness curls
  behind me, like a tail.

Peonies

Heart-transplants my friend handed me:
four of her own peony bushes
in their fall disguise, the arteries
of truncated, dead wood protruding
from clumps of soil fine-veined with worms.

"Better get them in before the frost."
And so I did, forgetting them
until their June explosion when
it seemed at once they'd fallen in love,
had grown two dozen pink hearts each.

Extravagance, exaggeration,
each one a girl on her first date,
excess perfume, her dress too ruffled,
the words he spoke to her too sweet—
but he was young; he meant it all.

And when they could not bear the pretty
weight of so much heart, I snipped
their dew-sopped blooms; stuffed them in vases
in every room like tissue-boxes
already teary with self-pity.

On the Wing

You fly to my table with unbuttoned sleeves.
You look like an angel with unbuttoned sleeves.

Where have you been? Did you run from a fire?
Here, share my meal with unbuttoned sleeves.

Like a page dipped in ink, your cuff's in my coffee.
You have something to tell with unbuttoned sleeves.

Don't say it yet. That's not what you mean.
I know you too well with unbuttoned sleeves.

How many years since I first loved your face?
You could have set sail with unbuttoned sleeves.

Clothes make the man. Our bed's still unmade.
Please pay the bill with unbuttoned sleeves.

Unbutton me back to our first nakedness:
I have no name at all with unbuttoned sleeves.

Crystal Ball

"Here's a story for you," he said. He slid the paper
off his chopsticks and snapped them, making two from one.
Then folded a red accordion from the wrapper,
pressed it between his fingers, let it spring
and slide across the table like a snake.
There were red snakes on our placemats too, and dragons,
monkeys and rats. "This story that I see
before me"—and he studied the zodiac's
combination plate of animals—
"occurs, how perfect, in the Year of the Horse.
In '54. Did you know the Japanese,
maybe the Chinese too, think it's unlucky
to be born in one of them if you're a girl?"

"I *was* born in '54."

"Right, I forgot!
But that's perfect too. Everything fits today.
I just took Val for her final sonogram.
Next comes the birth. I'd never seen her move—
my daughter. Today I saw my daughter swim
inside Val, fuzzily, for the first time.
We're used to seeing *anything* on TV,
so for a second that seemed almost normal."

"1999. Is this a Year of the Horse?
Is that what you're trying to say? I'm sure she's fine."

"Of course she is." He studied the mat again.
"We ride to the millennium on the back
of the Rabbit—see? Fertility!—and then
the Dragon's waiting for us at the gates
of the year 2000. That number sounded
impossible, didn't it, when we were kids?
Amazing that it's matched up with the only
chimera for any year, the Dragon . . ."

"So come on. What's the story, anyway?"

He sighed, took a gulp of tea; then sat up straight.
"I don't—I can't describe it. Last night, Val
and my father and I watched a video
from 1954. Or just a clip
from a home movie, made by a family friend
who'd had it saved on video. A surprise
for my mother's younger child, age 46.
It was the only record of my mother,
moving and breathing, that I've ever seen.
My mother who died when I was two, whose death
has haunted me more than anything—"

"I know—"

“because I can’t remember her. There she was.
Sick, on her last vacation, in Venezuela—
you like the exotic touch? It was as if
she was destined always to be worlds away—
and standing at the counter of some store,
trying out perfumes. You can see her lift
a bottle up, to study it like a doctor
checking an IV. No, she was happy.
She lifts the bottle, you can see her smile,
laugh, even, and say to Dad, *It’s beautiful*—
I mean you can read her lips. Of course, no sound.”
He raised his chopsticks, like a magic wand.
“What I would give to hear her! I must have played
those few seconds back a dozen times, as if
the next time, anytime, I’d hear her voice.
As if, I swear to God, I’d learn to crawl
inside that crystal bottle of perfume
like a little genie. As if in the end
I’d smell what my mother smelled.

“Imagine,” he went on,
“your mother says just one thing in your life,
and what she says is, *It’s beautiful*. You see?
But there was more. This morning I understood
how lucky I was. First I saw my mother move,
half a century after it couldn’t happen.
And then my daughter. I got to see her move—
the child you know I feared I’d never have

because I married late—and in a way
I saw her outside her lifespan, like my mother.
And all within the space of twenty-four hours.
On two TV screens! Nothing more banal.
I'd looked in my past and future crystal ball."

Our soup had come. Meanwhile, unwatched, the screen-
saver of the laptop I'd left on
at home was open, a window onto icons
of windows flying forward endlessly
like long-dead stars still seeking by their light
and at the speed of light a match in words.

"What do you think?" he asked. "Is it too neat
to write about? Would anyone believe it?"

"Probably not," I said, dipping a spoon
into the cosmos of my egg-drop soup,
and inhaling, as I leaned down, the aroma
of the moment's vapor. "Still. It's beautiful."

After September

Evening, four weeks later.
The next jet from the nearby Air Force base
repeats its shuddering exercise
closer and closer overhead.
A full moon lifts again in the fragile sky,
with every minute taking on
more light from the grounded sun, until
it's bright enough to read the reported
facts of this morning's paper by—
finally, a moon that glows
so brilliantly it might persuade us
that out there *somebody knows*.

A comfort once—the omniscience
of Mother, Father, TV, moon.
Later, in the long afternoon
of adolescence, I lay on the grass
and philosophized with a friend:
would we choose to learn our death date
(some eighty years from now, of course)?
Did it exist yet? And if so,
did we believe in fate?
(What *we* thought: to the growing
narcissist, that was the thing to know.)
Above our heads, the clouds kept drifting,
uncountable, unrecountable,
like a dreamer's game of chess

in which, it seemed, one hand alone
moved all the pieces, all of them white,
and in the hand they changed
liquidly and at once into
shapes we almost—no,
we couldn't name.

But if there were one force
greater than we, had I ever really
doubted that he or she
or it would be literate?
Would see into the world's own heart?
To know all is to forgive all—
(now, where had I read that?).
Evil would be the opposite, yes?—
scattershot and obtuse:
what hates you, what you hate
hidden in cockpits, caves, motel rooms;
too many of them to love
or, anyway, too late.
By now I've raided thousands
of stories in the paper for
thinkable categories:
unlettered schoolboys with one Book
learned by heresy and hearsay;
girls never sent to school;
men's eyes fixed on the cause;

living women draped in shrouds,
eyes behind prison-grilles of gauze.

Mine, behind reading glasses
(updated yearly, to lend no greater
clarity than the illusion
that one can stay in place),
look up and guess what the moon
means by its blurred expression.
Something to do with grief
that grief now seems old-fashioned—
a gesture that the past
gave the past for being lost—
and that the future is newly lost
to an unfocused dread
of what may never happen
and nobody can stop.

Not tired yet, wound-up, almost
too glad to be alive—as if
this too were dangerous—
I imagine the synchronized operations
across the neighborhood:
putting the children to bed;
laying out clean clothes;
checking that the clock radio
is set for six o'clock tomorrow,
to alarm ourselves with news.

An Open Book

for Agha Shahid Ali (1949–2001)

I saw your father make a book,
instinctively, from upturned palms;
  as prayers began
in a language I don't understand,
I saw he didn't need to look.

Your brother, sisters, others read
from lines in their own empty hands
  that you were dead,
or so it seemed to one who had
nothing by heart yet but the snow.

For days now, I've kept seeing how
the volume of your coffin sank
  into the sole
dark place in all that whiteness—like
your newest book of poems, blank

to you in your last weeks because
a tumor in your brain had blurred
  more than your eyes;
prompting your memory, a friend
had helped you tape it word by word.

After, at your brother's house,
I asked your father: "What does it mean
  when you pray with open
hands? Are they a kind of Koran?"
He smiled, and said I was mistaken:

he'd cupped hands to receive God's blessings.
Nothing about the Book at all;
    but since I'd asked,
here was the finest English version
(plucked up from the coffee table—

tattered cover, thick but small
as a deck of cards), translated by
    an unbeliever,
a scholar who'd found consolation
in it when he lost his son.

That was the closest the old man
would come to telling me how he feels.
    I think of him
when in my head a tape unreels
again your coffin's agonized

slow-motion lowering upon
four straps, incongruously green;
    and then that snap—
like Allah's blessings falling through
fingers that wished to keep you.

Acknowledgments

Thanks to the editors of the following magazines, where poems in this book first appeared, sometimes in slightly different form: "The Reader" and "After September" in *The American Scholar;* "Discovery" in *The Atlanta Review;* "A Morris Dance" in *The Atlantic Monthly;* "Advent" in *Harvard Divinity Bulletin;* "Trompe l'Oeil" in *The Kenyon Review;* "Hare" and "In the Guesthouse" in *The New Criterion;* "Midsummer, Georgia Avenue" in *The New Republic;* "Deliveries Only" and "Peonies" in *The New Yorker;* "Glasses" and "Florida Fauna" in *Profile, Full Face;* "Shadow" in *The Southwest Review;* "The Accordionist" and "For Emily at Fifteen" in *Stand;* "TWA 800" in *Upstairs at Duroc;* "The Newspaper Room" and "Another Session" in *The Yale Review;* "Office Hours" and "The Big Sleep" in *Columbia: A Journal of Literature and Art*. "On the Wing" was first published in the anthology *Ravishing DisUnities: Real Ghazals in English*.

I am grateful to the MacDowell Colony and to the Bogliasco Foundation for residencies that enabled me to complete this book. Madeleine Blais, Daniel Hall, Ann Hulbert, Brad Leithauser, Peggy O'Brien, Cynthia Zarin, and my editor, Ann Close, gave much-appreciated help.

"Peonies" is dedicated to Ellen Berek; "The Newspaper Room" to Isaac Cates; "Discovery" to the memory of Amy Clampitt; "After September" to Anne Fadiman and George Colt; "TWA 800" to Claire and David Fox; "A Morris Dance" to the memory of Harold Korn; "Shadow" to the Kundl family; "Trompe l'Oeil" to Mark and Bryan Leithauser; "Crystal Ball" to the Lyon family; "Office Hours" to Amanda Maciel and Diane Rainson; "Midsummer, Georgia Avenue" to Wyatt Prunty; "Erasers" to Albert Salter; "The Reader" to Marty Townsend.

A NOTE ABOUT THE AUTHOR

Mary Jo Salter was born in Grand Rapids, Michigan, and grew up in Detroit and Baltimore. She was educated at Harvard and Cambridge Universities and worked as a staff editor at *The Atlantic Monthly* and as Poetry Editor of *The New Republic*. Her awards include fellowships from the Ingram Merrill and Guggenheim Foundations. A vice president of the Poetry Society of America, she is also a co-editor of *The Norton Anthology of Poetry*. In addition to her five poetry collections, she is the author of a children's book, *The Moon Comes Home*. She is Emily Dickinson Senior Lecturer in the Humanities at Mount Holyoke College and lives with her family in Amherst, Massachusetts.

A NOTE ON THE TYPE

The text of this book has been set in Goudy Old Style, one of the more than one hundred typefaces designed by Frederic William Goudy (1865–1947). Although Goudy began his career as a bookkeeper, he was so inspired by the appearance of several newly published books from the Kelmscott Press that he devoted the remainder of his life to typography in an attempt to bring a better understanding of the movement led by William Morris to the printers of the United States. Produced in 1914, Goudy Old Style reflects the absorption of a generation of designers with things "ancient." Its smooth, even color, combined with its generous curves and ample cut, mark it as one of Goudy's finest achievements.

Composed by NK Graphics
Keene, New Hampshire

Printed and bound by United Book Press
Baltimore, Maryland

Designed by Soonyoung Kwon